WHAT STRANGER MIRACLES

James Brush

Coyote Mercury Press
Austin, TX

What Stranger Miracles

ISBN-13: 978-0-9849205-5-6

for Rachel & Silas

"To me the sea is a continual miracle,
The fishes that swim—the rocks—the motion of the
  waves—the ships with men in them,
What stranger miracles are there?"

—Walt Whitman, "Miracles"

CONTENTS

Thrown to Sea (I)

The ocean spits out plastic: faded, thin, but whole. The great-grandchildren of those who threw it in retrieve the relics, invent stories and religions for their ancestors, singing their praises only to go home and complain bitterly that they didn't leave behind something more useful than just the cast off detritus of their lives. Not even a boat to get off this rock. They are prisoners. The sea is the law.

THE SURVEYORS

The surveyors stand on the shoulder with their orange safety vests, rainwater swirling and pooling around them in eddies as it flows downstream. You'd think they were just measuring the highway, but they record everything: the caliber of the rifle in the gun rack and the carats in the diamond you tap on the steering wheel. They stare at you like they know everything about you. They probably do. They know what you're planning and where you'll go afterwards. But they don't tell anyone. They never will.

THE DIFFERENCE ENGINE

You will never know how hard it rained that day when the world became an ocean. The backhoe hit something solid. Fifteen road workers in muddy jeans and hardhats grumbled to a stop and stared at the great metallic wings among the fossilized shells. A storm chaser pointed at a tornado dropping a few miles off. *It's getting away*, he shouted. The oldest known human settlement in the Americas is just a few miles from here, but we raise our glasses to smaller wonders. In the morning, I bury yet another road-killed squirrel in the flowerbed.

EXTINCTIONISM

I started cutting back in '90. Carved *dusky seaside sparrow* on my arm when news of its extinction broke. Been at it ever since. Knives at first, but I'm saving for a laser scalpel. There's not much skin left and after *Bermuda saw-whet owl* took up half my thigh, I need something that cuts smaller lines. Kids ask for autographs in airports, and I oblige even as parents mumble, *Damn extinctionist.* There's not much space left on me. Strips of skin peel off and flop on the ground. The pages of a book left too long in the rain.

THROWN TO SEA (II)

It's an odd T-shaped island. Flying over, seabirds who've learned to spell can't help but look for other letters, an alphabet afloat on the overwhelming blue, but it's just that lone T, and the people, they are of the sea. They throw their best plastic in and watch the waves swallow all the evidence that they had lived. This is their sacrifice and preparation. The waves call them. The sea is Heaven.

THE WORLD IS A MAGNET

Compasses pull toward the heart, the pole star. This is
understood in the robot impulses of beetles. The world is
a cooling iron heart weakening with the eons, pulling
satellites and mariners off course while stars, constant,
look on as the sea laps the shore. We run down the sand,
dive in and swim home.

Beginner's Mind

She started collecting words as a little girl, gathering them in butterfly nets and bringing them home to show her parents. By high school she'd switched to symbols and signs. Things her family never understood. She wondered if horses knew about fish. Did equine visionaries imagine them and call it sci-fi? She wrote a symbol for this not-knowing and glued it to everything she owned. When she grew older she built a boat but couldn't name it. Her granddaughters would think of something.

Summoning

We learned the difference between boneyards and gardens of eternal rest the day we stumbled over ivy-covered headstones in the hour before sunset. Familiar surnames from the island's past lay scattered and toppled, poking through centuries of leaf litter, soft soil and old beer cans. Two broad-winged hawks carved spirals overhead as a little girl's cry for help disappeared into slow-moving water. An incandescent spark between two wires reveals dead snakes, spiders under a bridge, a raccoon scrambling away. Water is so full of memory and screams.

Ascent

Sinking deeper as the boat receded, she worked her chains. The world was locks and water, but she knew the key and smiled as she sank. Waves came and went leaving patterns in the surf. A message: *Help me.* The beach litter was a map of the seafloor. He swam for hours into the darkening sea, found her lying in the coral. *You came,* she said. He exhaled for the last time. The sea was air, the coral home. Their love the fish, the legs they grew as they evolved back to land to invent boats and chains, locks and keys.

THROWN TO SEA (III)

A leopard stalks the high slopes. At home in a thin-sky world on the blue edge of night, she pads over a landscape of fossils, old shells and ancient plastic embedded in stone. Her tail is a python pursuing her through the snow, telling lies and trying to throw her back to sea, but she maintains her balance, always. It's what she does. The sea is just a legend.

ADSEG
Author's Statement

Just as they separate ax murderers from regular ones, holding them out for special derision and lengthier sentences, we segregate prose poems from regular poems. They get their own labels and cells, a metal toilet and four hashmarks—one for each consecutive sentence—carved into the crumbling walls on some prison island surrounded by and so far from the sea. The prose poem wakes with the others but hesitates when they roll the doors. It knows it shouldn't enter the yard with the other poems, those sad misdemeanors that just got busted that one time they tried something big.

INFP (I'LL NEVER FIND PROFITABILITY)
About the Author

James Brush saw a career counselor and took the battery of aptitude tests hoping to hear he'd be a good ultrasound tech, marketing guru, or sorcerer. He sat in the waiting room smoking cigars with expectant fathers from the '50s. He considered the pipe wrench he'd picked up at Home Depot; he could try plumbing. A peregrine falcon on the window ledge tore apart a pigeon for her nestlings. A good omen? When the counselor called his name, he saw it in her eyes. *You'd make a fine teacher or maybe a poet. I'm sorry,* she added, *there's nothing we can do.* You can find him online at *coyotemercury.com*.

Acknowledgements, Etc.

Thank you to my wife Rachel whose support and love is a daily wonder and to my son Silas who never ceases to surprise and amaze me. I love you both.

My sincerest thanks to Dale Wisely and Howie Good, editors at White Knuckle Press, for first publishing this collection as a free online digital chapbook in 2016.

What Stranger Miracles was a 2017 nominee for the Science Fiction Poetry Association's Elgin Award.

Earlier drafts of some of these poems originally appeared on my site *Coyote Mercury*.

All photos by the author.

ALSO BY JAMES BRUSH

POETRY
Highway Sky
Birds Nobody Loves: A Book of Vultures & Grackles

FICTION
A Place Without a Postcard

CHAPBOOKS
Six October Stones
a gnarled oak 2010
a gnarled oak